my secret camera

my secret camera

Life in the Lodz Ghetto

Photographs by Mendel Grossman

Text by Frank Dabba Smith

GULLIVER BOOKS • HARCOURT, INC. • SAN DIEGO • NEW YORK • LONDON

introduction

It is sometimes argued that in the face of suffering as terrible as that recorded here, art has nothing to say. Mendel Grossman's photographs prove that the contrary is true—that a single image plucked from the chaos of history can move us to understanding no less than to compassion; that beauty is never absent from human beings, even at the worst of times; and that such beauty is not wasted on us.

For these are beautiful photographs. That may seem to make no sense. How can images of inhumanity be beautiful? These men, women, and children of the Lodz Ghetto—into whose eyes Grossman's photographs make us look with exquisite pity and affection, as into the eyes of people we love—have lost their liberty. They have been systematically enslaved, humiliated, herded, branded like animals, and compelled to wear that ancient symbol of Jewish shame, the yellow star. Ultimately, though they do not know it yet, they will be prepared like animals for slaughter. Where is the beauty in that?

Well, there is beauty in the circumstances of the photographs, for a start. Taken secretly and at great personal risk, with a camera hidden inside Mendel Grossman's raincoat, the photographs have for that very reason a nervous, heroic, agitated quality. They catch life in the ghetto as though by surprise, free of self-consciousness or posing, without anything coming between the watcher and the watched. This makes the photographs unbearably touching. If the young boy in the peaked cap is unaware of any camera, to whom is he turning his anguished expression? To us? Isolated, it would seem, from all humanity, a woman in a yellow star scrubs the streets. We observe her as from the vantage point of angels. She is seen. She is remembered. Thanks to the photograph, the cruel futility of her occupation is given meaning for all time.

Yes, these studies break the heart. God help us if there is ever a time when they do *not* break the heart. But they strengthen the heart, too—and here is more of the beauty I speak about—because they show the victimized finding reason to laugh and joke, finding community, and purpose even, in circumstances you would think too horrible to bear. In the end that is what Mendel Grossman's secret photographs record most vividly—his subjects' inextinguishable appetite for life.

—Howard Jacobson, author of *The Very Model of a Man*
and *Roots Schmoots: Journeys Among Jews*

I have a secret camera. I hide it under my raincoat. I have cut the pockets so that I can stick my hands through to use it. I open my coat just enough for the lens to peek out.

I have to take my photographs secretly because I am a captive in the Lodz Ghetto. Not even the bridges go anywhere else.

I must keep on taking pictures—how else can I tell the real story of the thousands of men, women, boys, and girls trapped with me in this terrible place?

I often stay up all night to develop film and to make prints of my secret pictures. I have a darkroom because my official job involves printing photographs of Jewish workers for their identification cards.
I also take photographs of Jews in the ghetto doing their work. Some of these pictures are stuck into special albums that we give to the Nazis. Our Jewish leaders think that the Nazis will let us live if we remind them again and again about how hard we work.

I have to wear a yellow star on my jacket because I am Jewish. The Nazis have ordered all Jews to wear these stars.

The Nazis hate us because we are Jewish.
They surround us with barbed-wire fences,
and they watch us, too. We are trapped
in a small space.

I secretly climb to the top of buildings to
take pictures of Nazi soldiers. My friends tell
me I shouldn't. They worry that the Nazis will
catch me. They also know my heart is weak
and I will become ill if I do too much. My own
pain does not matter. I must show what the
Nazis are doing to my people. My pictures will
tell the real story, even if I die.

Thousands of people pour into the ghetto every day. They come from places the Nazi army has conquered. They are confused and frightened. They have left behind everything that was familiar to them.

Nobody knows what will happen

from one moment to the next.

No one saw me take this picture. I took it from the inside of a building, looking down on the street. I shook with anger to see children harnessed to carts like animals. Here, people are slaves.

I'm determined to make copies of this photo. I will give prints to my friends and I will hide the negative. Someday the world will know the truth of how these innocent boys suffered.

A woman scrubs the streets.

Such a tiny bowl.

Such a filthy street.

When will our slavery end?

In order to survive, my friend Sasha embroiders swastikas for Nazi army uniforms. Her heart sinks each time she sews this symbol of hatred. Everyone in her workshop is exhausted. Sometimes they are too tired even to talk to one another during their short break. And they have learned that moaning about the soup doesn't make it taste any better.

Men line up for bread.

The wagon driver throws the loaves to them.

Each loaf has to last for seven days.

Everyone is hungry.

This young man has so little food,
and yet he shares it. In spite of our
suffering, we help and care for
one another. And this little girl still
wears a bow proudly in her hair.

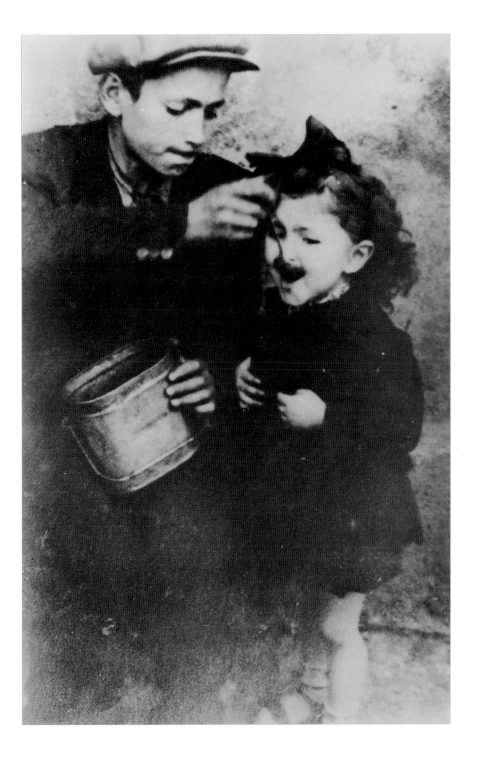

We used to bake matzos for Passover—
the Jewish festival of freedom—in Lodz.
But our own freedom has been taken away
by the Nazis. Still, though we are caged and
hungry, we must be brave and remain free
in our hearts.

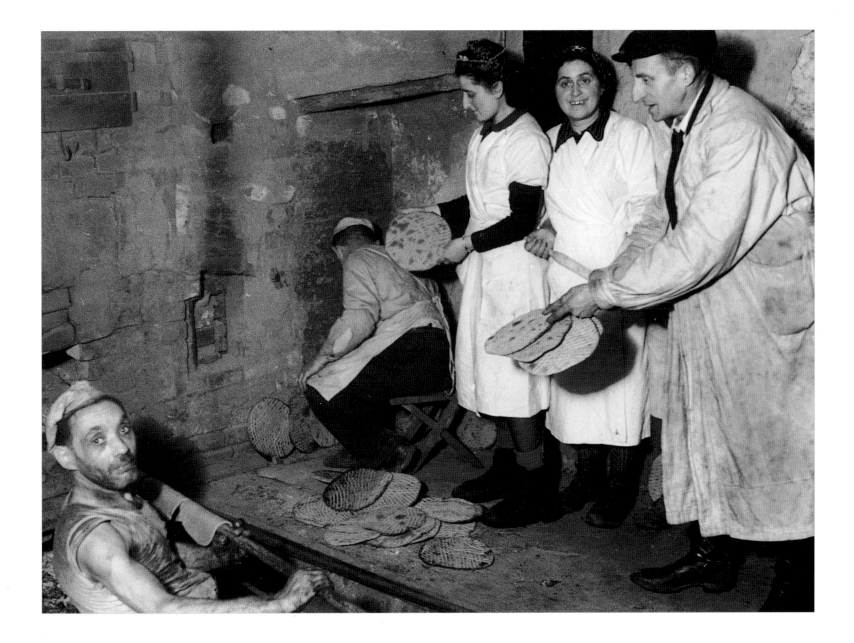

In spite of everything, we have to laugh
once in a while. We laugh at ourselves.
We make up funny songs, too.
Here Jankele, a tailor from Poland,
sings with Karol, a traveling salesman
from Austria.

My friends Aharon, Arye, Aveya, Franka, Mark, and Mirka, and my sister Roska, pose for a picture. They make me laugh, too.

Just as thousands of people are forced
to come into the ghetto, thousands are
shipped out.

No one ever comes back.

Time and again I witness children left alone,
torn from their families.

A mother to her son: "Be strong, my boy."

Will we ever see each other again?

a note about the photographer

Mendel Grossman was born into a Hasidic family in Lodz, Poland, in 1913. From a young age, he was devoted to drawing and photography. After the Nazis conquered Lodz on September 9, 1939, he was driven by a passion to bear witness to the human suffering that was going on around him. Undaunted by his own poor physical health, the deaths of loved ones, and threats from both Jewish and Nazi authorities, he produced a body of work that is unrivaled in its historical and artistic merits.

Shortly after occupying Lodz, the Nazis forced all Jewish residents to relocate to a cramped and filthy section of the city. The isolation of the Jews was complete when, on May 1, 1940, the Nazis sealed off the Lodz Ghetto from the rest of the city with barbed wire. Some 164,000 souls were trapped inside.

The Nazis set up a Jewish puppet government in the ghetto to carry out their orders. The ghetto became an urban slave camp. The Jewish leaders hoped that their efforts to marshal a productive labor force would spare ghetto residents from further barbarities.

Grossman found a job in the photographic laboratory of the ghetto administration. His official duties included photographing products of the ghetto workshops and taking identification pictures for work permits. This job not only allowed him access to film and darkroom supplies but also provided the perfect cover for his mission—to leave a day-to-day visual testimony of the tragedy enveloping him, and all those around him.

For four years ghetto residents were subjected to slavery, starvation, and periodic waves of deportation. In August 1944 most of those who had survived were sent to their deaths at Auschwitz. During these final days in the ghetto, Grossman packed tin cans, containing some ten thousand of his negatives, into a wooden crate, which he hid in the wall under a windowsill in his home. He had already distributed hundreds of prints in the hope that they, too, would survive.

Grossman himself was sent to a prison camp in Germany. Not long afterward he died on a forced march. According to his friend, Arie Ben Menachem, the artist-witness still had his camera with him.

After the Nazis were defeated in May 1945, Grossman's sister managed to locate her brother's hidden negatives and sent them to Kibbutz Nitzavim in Israel. Unfortunately, during the 1948 Israeli War of Independence, the kibbutz was ravaged by the Egyptian army and the negatives were destroyed.

However, not all of Grossman's work was lost. After the liquidation of the Lodz Ghetto, the Nazis kept some prisoners behind as slaves. Those slaves were forced to eliminate evidence of the existence of the ghetto. One of these men was Nachman Zonabend, a close friend of Grossman's. He managed to safeguard secret ghetto archives containing some of Grossman's photographs until the war's end.

After the war the remaining prints were collected and today they may be viewed at the Museum of the Holocaust and Resistance at the Ghetto Fighters' House in Kibbutz Lohamei Haghetaot, and at Yad Vashem, Jerusalem.

My Secret Camera was designed, edited, produced, and first
published in Great Britain in 2000 by Frances Lincoln Limited,
London, England

Library of Congress Cataloging-in-Publication Data
Grossman, Mendel.
My secret camera: life in the Lodz Ghetto/photographs by
Mendel Grossman; text by Frank Dabba Smith
p.   cm.
"Gulliver Books."
Summary: Photographs taken secretly by a young Jewish man
document the fear, hardship, generosity, and humanity woven
through the daily life of the Jews forced to live in the Lodz ghetto
during the Holocaust.
1. Jews—Persecutions—Poland—Lodz—Juvenile literature.
2. Holocaust, Jewish (1939–1945)—Poland—Lodz—Personal
narratives—Juvenile literature.   3. Holocaust, Jewish (1939–1945)
—Poland—Lodz—Pictorial works—Juvenile literature.
4. Lodz (Poland)—Juvenile literature.   [1. Holocaust, Jewish
(1939–1945)—Poland—Personal narratives.   2. Jews—Poland.]
I. Dabba Smith, Frank.   II. Title.
DS135.P62L64347   2000
940.53'18'094384—dc21   99-6268
ISBN 0-15-202306-2

First U.S. edition
F E D C B A

Printed in Hong Kong

The author would like to thank:
Judith Levine, photographic archives at Yad Vashem, Jerusalem
Zvi Oren, photographic archives at Ghetto Fighters' House, Israel
Cathy Fischgrund, Susan Posner, Judith Escreet, and Ellie Healey
at Frances Lincoln
Anne Davies, Ivan Holmes, and Nina Hess at Harcourt

For Cathy, Miriam, Lewis, and Sarah
—F. D. S.